D1394922

Willies
and
BOTTOMS

☆

by Purple Ronnie

First published 1999 by Boxtree
an imprint of Macmillan Publishers Ltd
25 Eccleston Place London SW1W 9NF
Basingstoke and Oxford

www.macmillan.co.uk

Associated companies throughout the world

ISBN 0 7522 1730 5

9 8 7 6 5 4 3 2 1

A CIP catalogue record for this book is
available from the British Library

Text by Giles Andreae
Illustrations by Janet Cronin
Printed and bound in Hong Kong

When you want your willy to be asleep...

a poem about
Droopy Bits

Drinking makes men get
all frisky
And chuck off their
clothes in a heap
They then want to Do It
like crazy
But find that their
Thingie's asleep

Men's Bits

Men's Bits come in all sorts of shapes and sizes...

... and there are millions of different words for them

Todger
Winkle
Doodah
Dangler
Goolies
Wobbler
Plonker
Zobber

a poem about

Men's Bits

Men's Bits sometimes look
like bananas

And sometimes like
shrivelled up grapes

But however they try

They just can't deny

That they come in the
silliest shapes

Tip for Girls

Men with big cars
hardly ever have
big willies

a poem about a

Trouser Snake

Men give names like
Trouser Snake
To bits they use in bed
But snakes are very big
I'd call them
Trouser <u>Worms</u> instead

Tip for Men

Remember always to keep your privates nice and clean

Tip for Willy Owners

It's not what you've got that counts...

...it's what you can do with it

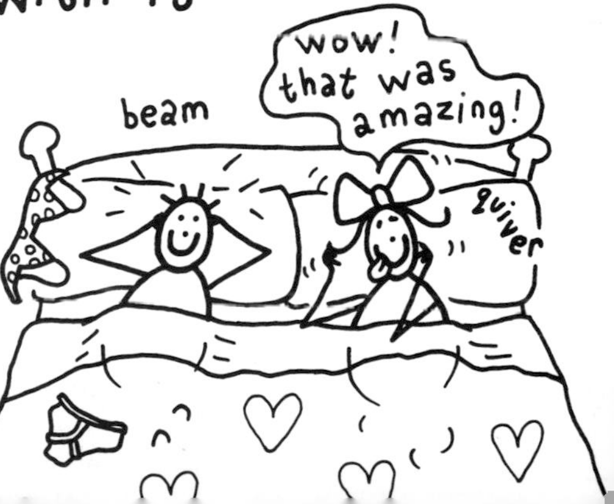

a poem about

Bottoms

Some people's bottoms are
skinny and small
And some are all fat and
enormous
Some are all hairy and
covered in spots
But yours is just totally
gorgeous

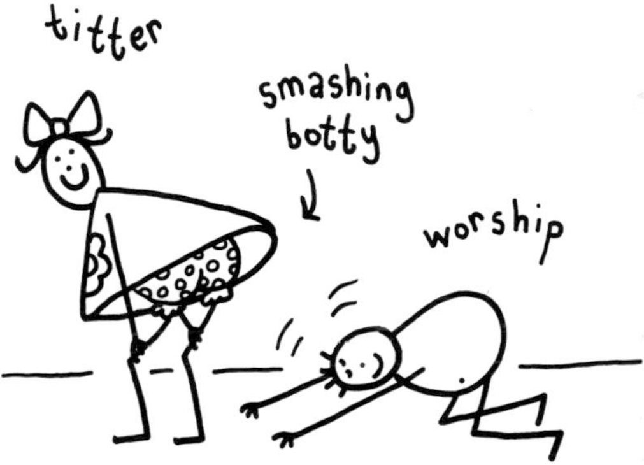
titter
smashing botty
worship

☆ Special Tip about Girls' Bottoms ☆

Always tell girls their bottoms are amazing

If you hesitate for a second-You've had it

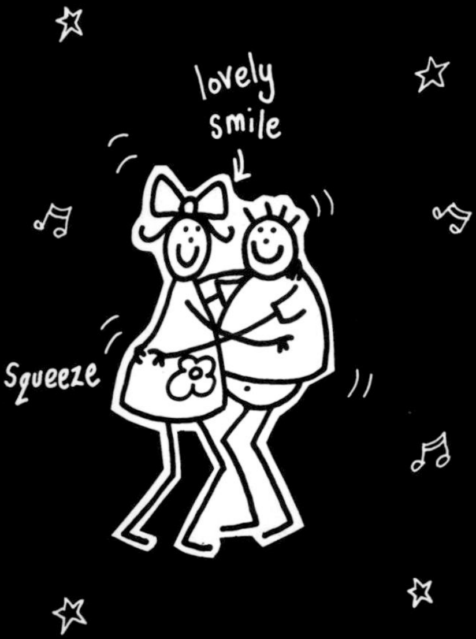
lovely smile
Squeeze

a poem about a
Squidgey Bum

Some people will do anything

To have a skinny bum
But what I like
Is a smiley face
And a nice fat squidgey
<u>Bum</u>

☆ Secret Note ☆

Front Bottoms

Only girls have Front Bottoms

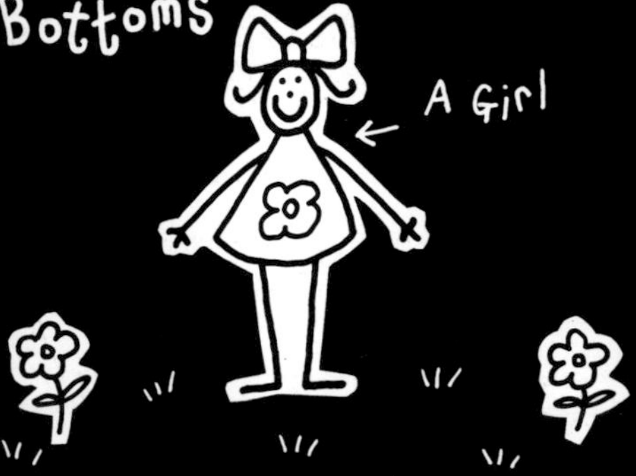

Front Bottoms are too rude to talk about...

...I just wanted to say it

FRONT BOTTOMS! FRONT BOTTOMS!

FRONT BOTTOMS! FRONT BOTTOMS!

FRONT BOTTOMS!

FRONT BOTTOMS!

FRONT BOTTOMS!

FRONT BOTTOMS!

The most amazing
thing you can do with
your bottom is
Bottom Burping

a poem about
↓
Bottom Burps

If your BOTTOM burps
in public
Try to say in time
"Goodness gracious
what a whiff
It doesn't smell like
mine"

Poo-eee
me running for it - having just done one
PFFRRT
scarper

Easily the most dangerous
is the Silent but Deadly

a poem about being

Silent but Deadly

They're silent as a tiny mouse
They do not make a sound
They warm up in your
                    trouser leg

Then waft for miles
                    around

First Rule of Bottom Burps

Your own Bottom Burps smell fantastic

another poem about

Bottom Burps

Some people screw up their
faces
And let out their farts
bit by bit
Some people hope that
they'll creep back inside
But it's great fun to let
them just rip

a poem about
The Lav

Of all the most fabulous
    things I can do
And the smashingest times
        I can have

There isn't a pleasure I love
        quite as much
As settling down on the Lav